Naming the Wind

Naming the Wind

Steven Rood

OMNIDAWN PUBLISHING
OAKLAND, CALIFORNIA
2022

Cover Photo by John Kleinhans

Cover typefaces: Albertus MT Std & Garamond Premier Pro.
Interior typefaces: Bernhard Modern & Garamond Premier Pro

Cover and interior design by Ken Keegan

Library of Congress Cataloging-in-Publication Data

Names: Rood, Steven, 1949- author.
Title: Naming the wind / Steven Rood.
Description: Oakland, California : Omnidawn Publishing, 2022.
Summary: "Wind moves through this book. Wind opens the poems: to the
dying beauty of the natural world; to the weathers inside the psyche and
without; to the connections between father and son, husband and wife, the
speaker to his mentor, the great poet Jack Gilbert."—Provided by publisher.
 Identifiers: LCCN 2022007679 | ISBN 9781632431042 (trade paperback)
Subjects: | LCGFT: Poetry.
Classification: LCC PS3618.O666 N36 2022 | DDC 811/.6 23/
   eng/20220--dc18
LC record available at https://lccn.loc.gov/2022007679

Published by Omnidawn Publishing, Oakland, California
www.omnidawn.com   (510) 237-5472
10 9 8 7 6 5 4 3 2 1
ISBN: 978-1-63243-104-2

For Marcia and Abbie

Not I, not I,
but the wind
that blows through me.

D. H. Lawrence

God came swiftly
on the wings of the wind.

Psalms, xviii. 10

Table of Contents

Naming the Wind

Khamsin is Arabic for the orange windstorm
that blows from the deserts across the Levant.
There are two Hebrew terms for the same wind:
Sharav (which appears in the Book of Isaiah);
and Ruach Kadim (Wind of the East).
The Khamsin is kin to the other great,
disturbing winds of the world: Diablo, Simoom,
Santa Ana, Chinook, Mistral, Terral, Bora,
Sirocco, Libeccio, Ghibli, Al Ol, Delta,
Etesian, Meltemi, Harmattan, Tremontana,
Berg, Aejej, Levantes, Shawondasee, Yamo,
Zonda, Brickfielder, Notias, Pittarak, Ostria,
Fohn, Carabinera, Mato Wamniyomi,
Crivetz, Elephanta, Garbis, Papagayos,
Vind Gnyr, Vind-Blaer, Hayate, Kadja,
Sirokos, Kohilo, Vardarac, Kona, Livas,
Boreas, Kubang, Landlash, Vorias,
Aturab, Mato Wamniyomi, Moncao,
'Inike, Kolawaik, Chi'ing Fung,
Pittarak, Ponentes, Quexalcoatl,
Samiel, Suestada, Maistros, Makani,
Sukhovey, Chocolatero, Bad-I-Sad-O-Bist-Roz,
Tokalau, Varda, Gregos, Haboob,
Mamatele, Vorias, Aquilo, Whittle, Xlokk.

By the Rivers of Babylon

I fell, hitting a greenstone boulder hard, tearing my elbow's skin.
The blood dried quickly in the heat, forming a small rust-dome.
I walked through orange air; its taste taught me one meaning of orange.
I kept looking down so I wouldn't trip again,
missing whatever was the new beauty above me in the smoke.
Stopped to drink, rest.
Nauseated, I tried concentrating on my breathing.
Reached a certain manzanita I'd known for thirty years.
Muscled trunk, brick-red made redder by the red sun.

Then I feel fists beating on the outside of my skull.
I fight off the fists.
At first I don't see the boy, attached to the fists.
When I do, he breaks through, beating me harder, and crying.
Is it for the trees combusting in the north? For us, both of us?
For the squadron of twenty-one turkeys overtaken by firestorm,
a turkey feather here, another, and then all of them ash?

Before I know I've let him, he crawls onto my chest, arms around me.
I bring my cheek to his hair, sit with his weight in my lap,
his weight about the same as my son's when he was six.

Conversation After the Ballet

27 bones of hand, 3 of arm, 26 of foot, chains of small bones,
the remaining 94, and a vast flexuous musculature holding them—
all impelled into flight. Music & the body.
The job least likely to be replaced by Artificial Intelligence
is Principal Dancer with the Canadian National Ballet.
Nothing except the actual body is a body.
The dancer is saying that a computer program learned how Beethoven
was Beethoven. Maybe, I say.
But can AI match a couple, hidden in Temescal Canyon,
moving smoothly under willows, circled by a hawk? No, she agrees.
Can AI speak in the language of spring on the mountain?
No algorithm can prove a ripe gooseberry,
a whispering flax, sun-detonated lilies.
Odors, qualities of light, rhythms now hidden beneath memory.
Emerging from stiffness, as one finds grace in an arm.
Matchless singularities. We look so small at table.

Self-Portrait with a Cod's Head

The man looks at himself, from above
and at an angle, sees
an old man, too old to be bothered by admirers or haters
who know nothing about a cosmos within.
The man puts the horrible head on a white plate,
fork and spoon in his hands, ready.
Cheeks, brain, collar, bones.
The cod's eyes look out, seeing
more than the man ever will see.
The man eats.
Oily flesh. Delicious.

Black Diamond Mines

Bushwhacking, crawling under, climbing up.
Hand over hand, crack by crack,
to the red sandstone pinnacle of Manhattan Canyon.
This is where my son will scatter my ashes.
I remind him every time we come here.
Here, I deposited into him all that I'd been able to glean
from rocks, brush, flowers, north winds, dusk.
When we're near the top, pressing through tough,
pokey chamise, parting branches, feeling them whip back,
I decide to press into a sharp branch to feel its sting.

Fermata

The fermata says *wait.*   So, for once, I take it seriously,
holding the rest beyond what is reasonable,   and beyond that
into something wild.   Staying out there in the wind
as people call for me to get down and play
the next thing.   Letting silence increase silence,
until the audience is furious,   and I'm shaking with doubt.

But can I deny the rare tingle and ease in my hands,
suspended between furies,   when they move like deer,
unforced and fluent up the slope?

Only my son knows how something settles on me
when we're walking, and I stop,   and we're quiet.
What if all anyone ever knows of my soul is its shining
interval of silence?   What if all they ever have of my music
is the *rest*?   Not words or notes, but the after and before,
coming from the precision of that silence?
What if I stayed with that unborn thing in me?
Entering possibility   like a cool, limitless sea,
believing anything can happen there   under the power of my hands?

Mr. Weiss

Clear as blue air washed by sparkling needle-clusters of pines—
the forty-carat blue diamond (with one crack),
still in its matrix of black rock.

The man only partly finished the stone,
which he keeps in a drawer, wrapped
in a handkerchief.

He's a specialist in cutting through
to the inclusions and flaws we spend a lifetime with
but almost never see.

He disappears from himself for hours, which might be years in the desert,
where none of us admits we died of thirst long ago.
For this man, the mirage of a pool is real.

He knows that for any stone to be whole,
it must be cut precisely at the lines of its imperfection.

Map of My Body

My toes reside in Silver Lake, clenched like fists.

Here is the itchy patch on my back, located in Golders Green,

where I became an artist, at twenty, and which I'm still scratching.'

On the subway platform at Court Street, I said to my girlfriend,

"Marriage: why not?" My wife of thirty-six years is now situated

in the Twin Temples of Groin and Stomach.

The terrified boy-I-was still hides in the San Fernando Valley,

which bursts forth from my peachy heart at inappropriate times.

I was first born into the colored spirals of Bach's fugues

in my Berkeley dorm room.

My father's deathbed is in Hollywood, which I keep forever

as my feeling function at the base of my brain.

I am the former boy, now man, soon to be old, then dead,

here and there, *saecula saeculorum*, past, present, future—

all times and places housed in my left hand, where I currently reside.

I dwell in the canyons of Agua Dulce, whose streams enwrap

my sturdy donkey-feet,

and in arroyos of Anza Borrego, during seasons of repose and agitation,

where I often sleep in a light tent.

My fury at charlatans, hustlers, con-men, blusterers, and coercers

burns my throat, which lives in North Hall,

where I first read Antigone and Lear.

The Santa Monica mountains of my youth are still here in my nose,

scent-struck by sage.

Affections without border or limit. Durable.

Marked clearly between my nipples, the permanent Bethlehem

of all my interior lives. My endless suffering over my flexuous family
lodges in my mouth, which is Minsk, Odessa,
The Wilderness of Zin. The mouth that has redeemed
a hundred generations of my people that came before me
and will illuminate, if I'm lucky, two generations to come.

Behind My Ribs

Inside the ventricles of my left hemisphere.
Jewel of the sagging-light-afternoons.
Song so finely tuned it comes with a little dance
and bracelets of yellow bakelite.
Cabbage roses showering petals on my soaked face.

Inside the old building, in the half-light of a stairwell.
Here, where the echo is strongest,
everything I whisper comes back as a shout.
The silence outside kissing the silence within,
and the small shining where they touch.

Montara Beach

Winter sea on my right, bald coastal mountains on my left.
Past white llamas, a stinky paddock.
My legs heavy at first, aching;
then shifting to a smooth, painless stride.
A body forgiving its age. Age forgiving its body.

I remember last month, before I closed my office for good,
I was alone in the stairwell with my guitar, late,
and rather than going home,
I revived a piece I hadn't played for years.
Prelude, Fugue, and Allegro in D Major by J.S. Bach.
It came easily, by dint of the music that had nested whole,
intact, ready in my fingers.

I'm running now,
fluently moving from my regular body to the alternate body inside me.
Running-music, sex-music, music-music—
held and released again into the alternate earth and sea.

Studio City

A creek runs down from hills to the flats. Laurels, walnuts,
tule marshes. Tongva-tribe grinding holes in boulders.
Then came the Spanish mission. Mexican ranchos.
Gene Autry's Spanish-style gated mansion. His horse.
Movie people. A small downtown. Feed store.
Bond's Market. Thrifty Drug Store, with soda fountain.
Clark Dennis Books. Dupars for pies.
Republic Studios. My shul. My school. My house.
Dust and heat. Birds. A private canyon of seeps,
trickles, shade, silence—where I hid.
Garnets studding a grey schist outcrop.
I went away. Came back when my mother died.
Almost all of it built over.
One towhee, a bush fluttering with skipper moths,
the hill behind the house, the smell of dusk.
This is not nostalgia. It is something I *possess*.
A place not longed for, but *here*.
The broken down house next door to my childhood home,
still smelling of Oletha's oil paints.
The stubborn ruin of it.
An incidental patch of the beginning, tough and un-square.
So this is like desire, but not quite.
Because desire wants the radiant absence, the loveliness turning away.
But I have the bitter and the sweet of it *now*.
I say *Scrape deep*. The smell fresh in my fingernails.

Hexagram 63 / After Completion

I told Mighty McGritchie's father I was a pianist and could play
Debussy's Claire de Lune. I was seven. He a big Hollywood composer.
He asked me what else I knew. Beethoven's Moonlight Sonata.
"Play, if you're so good," he insisted. I sat down, wiggled my fingers
in the air above the keys. Years later, practicing in solitude,
I grew into a guitarist, playing Bach and the Spanish *vihuelistas*.
The man is long dead, and now, as I'm an old man, fury arrives
unexpectedly with the Moonlight.

Gridley, California

Farmers grow prunes, walnuts, almonds
in orchards. Buttercup, filaree, poppy
sprout around the white-painted trunks.

We've come to meet Bob Stocksdale,
who turns walnut burls on his lathe
into bowls so thin they are lit amber.
Swirls of dolphins and fern fronds.

His trained crow walks up my arm
to my shoulder on its devil's feet.
Bob feeds us prunes, almonds, walnuts.

Laura and I go for a float along the irrigation canal,
canopied with long strands of blackberry flowers.
We slip down weirs and finish in a meadow,
where we lie under oaks.

Fifty years later, the air in summer
rusts with heat, smoke, exhaust, pesticide.
Farmworkers sicken. Everybody is high.
I want to leave nothing out.

Holding On

What is that tiny bird?
With coal-black skull cap,
nape and chest?
Chickadee? Junco?
Isn't a chickadee's call
"chick-a-dee"?
My birder-friend Bill
might have known. Or not.
He was really not
a serious birder.
But it would have been nice to ask,
him sitting by me on the bench.
Little beings, chipping
and trilling.
Bill's lumpy ashes
in a carton.
I'm alive, encircled
by chickadees (or juncos),
sparrows, a crow, bushtits, finches.
Pink magnolia blossoms loll.
A toddler looks up and points.

The Beginning

Started smoking weed, listening to jazz, Wilson Pickett, Otis Redding.
Jammed blues guitar every night. Got busy being in love with Laura.
Slid behind on the freshman assignments. Tried to catch up
by combining many topics into one paper.
Edmund Burke, Freud, plus Euripides.
The Federalists, Malcolm X, plus Lear.
Organized them by lining quote-cards up on the floor, then shuffling.
At the end of term, I gave a recital of the music I'd been playing
instead of doing the assignments. Bach's Prelude and Fugue in D major.
A Dowland fantasia. A Couperin passacaglia.
Professor Tussman said he would have flunked me but for the Bach.
Professor Kennard said that my synthetic mind was an evident delight.
Professor Tussman said that I was slovenly but talented
and might write something useful some day.

Sky Funeral

Vulture is delicate, with tiny hairs on his pink, naked head.
Big eyes, an intelligent nose sensitive to odors of flesh.
Vulture's shoulders are humped up, he walks awkwardly,
stooped over. When he flies, he rarely needs to work at flapping.
He lives in a companionable group, which croaks softly or hisses.

I almost never look at the etching of Vulture,
even though it's in front of my desk.
Just the way everything I'm first shocked by
recedes, becoming background, invisible.
Today, Vulture seems to wake in his frame
because Neil, my first analyst, loved birds.
Ducks, eagles, vultures, especially.
Vultures came to clean him away.

Argument Against the Reductionist View of Consciousness

Out of the slick mud at the bottom of the pond;
   Out of the muck of cattail root-scum;
Out of salamanders, frogs, the horrible carp;
   Out of slime and dung; Out of cloud-shaped pond-deeps;
Out of cow-wallows and the stink of bears;
   Out of algae-scum, rank watermeal;
Out of coontail, pondweed, purple loosestrife;
   Out of the anal glands of Morris Wachtel's beavers,
their castoreum and urine; Out of the gelatin
   extracted from boiled hides, tendons, cartilage,
ligaments, horns, and bones of Johnson's cows;
   Out of fallen and rotting aspen, larch, birch;
Out of saprophytic fungi and heart-rot;
   Out of punky, decaying touchwood;
Out of the deliquescence of *Coprinus comatus*—
   come this afternoon's spider webs,
mandalas of burning platinum droplets.

The Adventure

Shaking hands virtually—portals to occult interiors.
Permission to voyage steadily into another's eyes.
Pre-sexual amazement at cheeks, chins, hands, necks, mouths.
The privilege to ask questions.
(Usually only lawyers have the right.)
The delicate shifts among courtesy, modesty, lying.
Then surprising courage to say things
I'd even hidden from therapists.
Then the hot arc in the space between two strangers.
Nothing will come of it. Everything already has.

Linked

with open mouths, in public,
the way we'd kiss on streets just for the happiness.
Why did you arrive, after decades?
Is it the same magnetic sensitivity that swallows have
when they flutter unerringly back
to their mud nests every spring?
Partners in sparked neuronal webbing?
A tugging, deep in the limbic,
a lunar and polar pull in both our spines?

My Work

A foot-long spike
with hooks and beaks of iron and ivory.
The other is a russet-veined,
cordate-leaved, basal-rosetted herb,
out of which arise puff-clouds
of fringed pearls, netted in silk.
Each is restricted to its hidden scarp,
and each is the last of its tribe.
The oligarchs are playing a game.
Which one will win the right
to extirpate the plants' habitats
with towers bearing his name?
The oligarchs don capes
fitted with scarlet and yellow feathers
of now-extinct honeycreepers,
and sue each other in five courts
on three continents, until one
will get bored, the other prevail.
I receive my instructions from afar,
a slender voice from a lily's throat.

Work

In my office at the end of the day,
things wait beside me in the semi-dark.
Like animals sleeping. On my desk
the miscellany that somehow adhered to me.
Cigars I'll never smoke. An etching of an ancient olive tree.
A poor watercolor of Marian Gage's green cabin near a sycamore
in what is now Santa Monica. Shards of marble from Paros,
a terra cotta head of Aphrodite.
A postcard of Chagall's poet asleep amid chickens.
The poet, if he were to open his eyes,
would see me singing to myself after hours,
one hand holding a fistful of colored balloons,
the other hand holding my own tightrope.

"I Am a Human Being; Touch Me."

A thousand meetings come to nothing.
Of one meeting, everything can come.
If I don't look at each face carefully,
I will surely miss the important one.
By sleepwalking, or grouping by race,
I will lose the paradise I could enter forever.
This human work requires precision.
Kali wears her necklace of skulls.
I wear a necklace of elephant hearts.

When I Stand in the River

Slabs of lumber, brush, bodies, cars, mud, other debris push past.
The second I put one foot out sideways, cross-current,
or let my fingers drag in the rush, I feel surge,
and it punishes me. Flays my skin, thuds my groin,
makes me wish I hadn't dared to send out my snail-pip feelers.
Nevertheless, against the river, I find my shape, stinging with isolation.
Born into myself that way through resistance.

Ruins

Cocteau was asked what he would save
if his house were burning. "The fire."

My house is burning.
I will save my guitar as the fire eats its body.

I smell the particular woods it was made of,
there in Granada in 1962. Rosewood, ebony, spruce.

I smell the odor of the first burns as Alva kissed me
after I played and sang for her Dowland's *Sorrow*.

I feel how the thin threads of nerves burned in my hands
when, at nineteen, I played the *fantasias* of Milan, the fugues of Bach.

I no longer need to play the burned instrument
in order to hear it breathe next to my chest,

its warmth remaining there as a stamp in soft metal.
I keep the ruin of it near my desk,

so I can smell the residue of its shape
as I type the memories of what it was like to burn with it.

Hexagram 30 / The Clinging, Fire

Johnson pastures about thirty milk cows. He knows the names
and personalities of each. He loves them, for they provide warmth
in the cold dawn of the milking shed. They chew solemnly
and have long tongues that wrap around Johnson's hand.
They yield cream twice a day, without fail, from bags and tubes
hanging between their bony legs. The cows walk in groups,
mostly facing the same way in a field.

My son's favorite heifer has blemishless red hair with a small
pompadour between her ears. She walks alone to the fence
where the boy comes every day with hands full of grass.
She sniffs, rumbles, stretches out her neck, moves her great head
through the electric wires, lets my son scratch her ears.

   Care of the cow brings good fortune.

Cows have close friendships within their herd. Cows remember.
When hayfields dry away in the growing heat of the earth, stressed
cows will first stop making milk. Then they'll lick their farmers' faces
and die.

Lilian Pond, Catskills

Swifts whirr around the man's head.
        The splash of his son's feet
    as the boy hunts the pond for salamanders with orange spots.

The breeze pushes the pond towards the man. Small waves
insisting in a language not Hebrew, not Ugaritic, not words,
    but something that comes before.

        His son's feet are perfect.

There Came a Wind

An eighth-inch below the grass is blackness for eight thousand miles.
On the planet's surface are squirrels, finches, crows, dogs, dog-walkers,
the parts of trees that sway.
The upper world is busy with animal and human politics.
The underworld is busy with moles chewing and digging
through the lawn, who, via their small tunnels,
allow me to get on my hands and knees and gaze into the earth.
We all ride lightly on vast lakes of liquid nickel and iron.

I remember my first Cretan melon.
Its weight and rough skin. The heat of the island.
A faint odor that smelled nothing like bread, tomato, cucumber, onion.
The cut of the woman's knife exposing pale green flesh.
Cavity and seeds. A vegetal geode.
Juice dripping.
A single melon's interior that had never before been seen
or relished.

Luis De Milan

Lived in Renaissance Spain after the Reconquista.
He composed for the court. Was adept at the *vihuela*,
a lovely, quiet, early guitar, shaped like a young torso.
He was also a poet. He titled his book *El Maestro*.
I began playing the six easy *pavanas* when I was thirteen.
They felt square, with block-like chords.
When I was seventeen, I undertook the difficult *fantasias*—
combinations of simple modal chant-lines
and running embellishments in marvelous variations.
I didn't understand them for the next fifty years.
When I turned seventy, I slowed them down.
Allowed them. Milan wrote, *Now there came a wind*.

Squirrels

It's taken nine months for the squirrels to recognize
my particular human shape— I am the peanut tosser.
We sit next to each other on the grass so close I hear them chew.
The thin, skittery one with feathery ears and a koala's face;
the robust one, with nice girth, berry-eyes, lush fur.
They have hard lives being chased by dogs, who almost never win.

Forty years ago, I visited a mercury mine, the New Idria,
in the Diablo range. I'd come as a representative of the auctioneer
hired to sell off its remains— rusted mine carts, crushers, hammers,
picks, huge ovens for cooking ore. I met the last caretaker,
who offered me his "varmint stew" for lunch.
Milk, potatoes, squirrels.

The Worm

The worm eats dirt and fungi, his humble provender.
The worm's father teaches him that he is a born-worm,
who must blindly serve his worm-progenitors and be bait.
The worm's segments and long muscles enable him
to push through soil. He has no voice. He shares this silence
with all worms. And these fates: sliced by shovel, drowned in rain,
plucked by robin, squished under boot. It's eat, tunnel, undulate, shit.
Lucky, he muses. Today, the worm is eating along in loam,
under camellias, from nowhere to nowhere. He tastes a flake of gold,
then a nugget of raw gold. Nothing had ever tasted like that.
He still cannot be heard, but he is singing gold to himself.

Getting Close

Five squirrels are chewing the peanuts I tossed.
I'm lying on my back on the lawn.
I am especially attached to two of them—
the one whose tail was burned off and the one who runs up
and lets me touch his dry, tan nose, which allows me to imagine
I'm riding the earth,
letting its great center pull me down.
So much easier being flat than walking:
gravity cannot hurt me.

Squirrels are contra-gravity, flying up trunks.
As are crows. As are kids floating in the public pool.

Something is going on deep in the earth.
It is making sapphires, citrines, rubies.
Maybe I'll turn to dust and befriend the wind.

In My Voice, a Language
I Had No Choice but to Speak

Hollywood English flavored by Yiddish, Hebrew, onions, palm trees,
and out of which I only *think* that I create a world.
My body, a late arrival from ancestors stretching back in time
to tabernacles in the wilderness.
Even my name is syllables hummed to me by others.
Almost all of me
given.

And out of the given, I have but a slender edge of invention.
I, therefore, to the greatest extent of my agency, in my seventieth year,
repudiate, abandon, cancel, deny, annul
all the prohibitions, vows, promises, oaths
that have been heaved onto me.
Vows no longer my vows, prohibitions no longer my prohibitions,
oaths no longer my oaths.
If there is freedom, I exercise it now.
To find my regular form,
a disturbing surprise to myself.

Hanukah Party

All the party-ers tonight are limping,
complaining, tapping their hands.
Rustics, remnants, the mostly elderly
come out for companionship on a dark afternoon
to hear music from somewhere between Romania,
Transylvania, and the Carpathian Bow.
A klezmer piece always begins with a wailing, plodding drone,
then splits open into polyrhythmic death-life-dances.

I bless the luck of reaching this time, alive or half-alive, with this tribe.
We are not a free people and maybe will never be free
of the unseen weights pressing our bodies, bending them down.
I wonder what outsiders will think of the Jews,
the bad dancing, the out-of-tune soulful music
that gives little jolts of forgetting and memory together.
Forgetting the misery. Remembering the misery.

Apostate

Rabbi Zimmer was relieved of his pulpit
for sleeping with a married woman,
an alto in the temple choir.
"I entered the rabbinate with no faith,
and it has ended with indifference and relief,"
he told the committee. He looked ridiculous
from a distance and at an angle, the way we all do,
pretending to be something coherent, with rectitude.
He was a thousand guppies in a bucket.
All he really liked about being a Jew, Rabbi Zimmer said,
was his grandparents' memories of Yonah Shimmel's pickles,
the smell of cabbages, a small pot of meat in Mrs. Burstein's kitchen.
And his own memories of the Torah's silver crown, its tinkling bells,
his astonishment at finding youthful lovemaking in the Song of Songs,
the sourness of Ecclesiastes, the triumph of Job over God.
He was judged an *apikoros*, a heretic, an abomination.
Still, *Jew* is big enough to hold him.
The choir sang the Yiddish song *Dona Dona*.
In Rabbi Zimmer's English version:
"Because calves are easily bound and slaughtered,
some Jews become swallows,
skimming the pond at dusk for flies.
How the winds are soughing.
Sough and sough the whole day through
and half the summer's night."

Taxonomy

"This is my favorite lichen, I haven't seen it for over a year,"
I heard the young woman telling her companion on Twin Peaks.
I too know this lichen: an orange crust next to pistachio-green, flat,
peony-like lichens covering exposed chert and greenstone.
I was so happy to hear somebody call out a lichen,
and not agonize over computers or bad relationships,
which I do enough of.

Once I saw here a father and son carrying huge, billowing butterfly nets.
When I asked, they told me that they had found thirty species that day.
(I knew five: monarch, swallowtail, cabbage, skipper, mourning cloak.)
The other hikers I'd seen were two birders calling out "flicker"
and "bushtit." I myself seek the odorous fungi and plants,
along with elegant orange lichens, hawks, vultures.
These people and I are a "cohort of peculiar eccentrics."
In taxonomy, the name for members of the same species.

Nevertheless

The *dybbuk* hands me fate. Hands me work
requiring utmost skill, to be used only with honesty
and for huge stakes. Hands me dying parents.
A teenage son. A marriage.
Dybbuk tells me to stay with all of them, serving,
not running away. And not just going
through the motions.

Someone is bleeding to death before me,
and I must help. *But I don't know how*, I say.
Still the *dybbuk* wants me to do my best.
No cheating, no flippancy, no routine.
And he requires faith. Faith?
Even with the end in sight, dybbuk insists.
Otherwise the Devil will catch you.

My *dybbuk* delivers wounds, evil, money, love, and mountains.
Tells me I'll never understand any of them.
Nevertheless, he says. And hands me more,
making me watch frailness come to loved ones.
Finally it begins to feel different.
How else can I explain what happens downstairs,
very early, as colors begin shyly in the kitchen?

Walk #3410

A sycamore tree next to the scrap metal yard.
Every day I come to stand in the cold
falling from its swaying.
Even on the hottest afternoons, I'm a leaf amid leaves.
Workers are busy sorting metals.
I'm invisible. Almost as invisible as when I'm in the woods,
talking to myself, singing off-key with my eyes closed,
ignored by the wrentits and towhees.
I wonder how my lawyer friends survive their jobs.
How can they maneuver from task to task all day, none finished?
A few times I've tried to bring them on a walk.
Mostly they shrug, meaning "Too busy, what can I do?"
I tell myself there's really nothing anybody can do.
Still, I think, maybe we have a reservoir
of silence, like the desert is. Even if we've gone there
only once, when we were young, we carry that thing in us
seeping out from inside to join itself, without our trying.

Obligation

The Polish poet Zuzanna Ginczanka comes to me in a dream.
The Germans arrested, tortured, killed her.
She has fared well enough in death, these eighty years.
Only slightly puffy in face, she's eating a cheese sandwich.
My blood will bind these fibers with fresh down
and thus transform these winged ones to angels.
I tell her that I can't write anything important here in America.
Forgive yourself you were born, and your happiness.

Amadeus

This morning, Piano Concerto No. 20 reached the portals
of my cranium. Then entered.
Three, four hummingbirds—
iridescent teal, ruby— fanned my eyelids.
Their colors detonated.
I began to type this poem,
which changed over many drafts
until I'd replaced almost everything,
doubting what was left.
I thought about the ballet.
How the godly dancers come out of the North Stage Door
to become small, skinny humans again. To-and-fro.
Then I heard how, after the agitation of the orchestra,
Mozart's piano's answer begins *pianissimo*.

The Junior Bach Festival

Light beams down on Michelle Kim's head,
flows through her, and comes out her nine-year-old fingers
as the Partita in E Major. Her face flushes,
then goes beyond sweating to glowing.
The piece accelerates, faster than the impossibly small hands
can hold, when she stops midway, stands straight,
and walks off. Sherri Wang, twelve, is next
with a gavotte. Newton thought light
was made of colors. Goethe said light
was dark in the evening and burned white
on marble at noon. Either way, when it fills us,
spoonful by golden spoonful,
whatever is in our mouths is singing.

Having, and Having Again

We'd never been out of Hollywood. Or seen snow
or pines or a lake that wasn't formed from concrete, like Silver Lake.
My father drove us to a small, borrowed cabin at Lake Arrowhead.
My sister and I played in the back seat all the way,
through the new kinds of trees, blurs with upright brushes.
My father had a key. Opened the wood door to the odor
of wood smoke that the whole, cold room smelled of.
Which would become my foundation scent
that all other odors were measured against for my long life.
He started a fire for us. My sister and I ate sandwiches
and played in the snow. A lifetime later we are busy remembering,
as we do on our Sunday calls. She tells me how that wood smoke
had also been her first memory of scent,
how we'd been penetrated by the same mystery.

Two Birds in Spring

Poppy, suncup, lilac, iris, toothwort.
I reach down for them here in the Botanical Garden.
Two Cooper's hawks call to each other *Kee'eer, Kee'eer, Kee'eer.*
The male, with spotted-cream breast and banded tail,
flies to the female, touches her crown with his talons.
Wheeling, crying across the canyon into a redwood grove, the pair
carry my eyes outside myself for an instant.
What other are they, what other might I be?
I bend to steal an apricot-colored chanterelle,
only the fourth one I've seen this dry year.
Talk-sing to a squirrel, who puts up with me for a few seconds.
Breathe in the scents of the four sages: blue, purple, black, white.
My wife is laid up with a fractured knee.
I will bring her the early spring odors that we both most need.
I will crush to dust the fragrant, volatile, primitive scale-leaves
of a pygmy cypress in my fingers.
The scent will last just long enough.

Exodus, Lost Chapters

Bricks, mortar, straw.
Killing of babies.
Nile stinking of blood.
Darkness. Boils.
Escape to the wilderness,
little food, little water,
and that little, bitter.
Prophets point. People grumble.
Me understanding only
that fire will scream up my nostrils
and burn out my brain
if I get the sacrifice wrong,
according to somebody.
Stars spraying out of crags.
The words I speak in the desert—-
husks around the void.
I see the eyes of my son, my wife.
Of ibex. Hoopoe. Goat.
We're in a small sleeping circle,
glowing with agate and lapis.

Locust Tree in the Courtyard

A woman walks by, carefully
noticing the elderly men on a bench.
First it's their eyes, then their heads.
Seeds from the tree cascade down
and she seems to walk through snow flurries
without being touched.
She is making weather.
Golden seeds fall
in the wind and tremble
on the cement near the bench.
Loneliness hatches her seeds
into the old men's lungs.
The courtyard is full of beauty.
What is that? Like what?

What I Did

Looking into the cavity of a raw chicken, I am looking
into my mother's throat.
I reach in and pull out my mother's liver.
It had been two weeks since I'd begun feeding my mother's open mouth
morphine from a dropper.
She was a chick, just born, with a wild dog scrabbling
at the door of the hen house.
He'd be inside in a moment.
The hospice nurse came each day to my mother's bedside
and told me how to administer the doses and the signs to look for.
Blotching of skin, trumpeting breaths, restlessness,
sudden peace.
I kept doing what I think the nurse said, and watching.
My mother at last pulling away the oxygen, turning from me,
private, at the very end.
I would never be innocent again.

Marriage

On the trail to Twin Peaks, I pass a woman in a mask.
She says something muffled about "many termites ahead."
I say "Beetles?" thinking that beetles, not termites,
bore the soft pinewood. "No, termites," she says.
I keep looking for a rising silver cloud of wings.
Nothing. Maybe I've lost my touch at seeing.
Then I find them: ten or fifteen turkeys
eating quietly amid the wild oats.

Elena, 1975

On Benton Street we kissed the first time—
a dry, grazing, partial kiss, then wet.
We were two fluids swirling in a clear bowl.
For a short time, I was vast deserts, colossal wrecked mountains—
that are what I could only understand
if they had above them the night skies.
It was August. Were her eyes blue or green?
Green, yes. A gray-blue-green that only night resembles.
Did it really happen?
I've witnessed miracles before.
The thousands of orange ladybugs massing
on a tree trunk, warming each other.
They were clicking and whispering, as *Seraphim* do.

Hexagram 61 / Inner Truth

A crane calling in the shade.
Its young answers.
I have a goblet.
I will share it with you.

My son and I are a hinge and bowspring of superior grace.

Let's see how this lily works.
First, we cut the swelled seedpod
to examine ovary and ovule.
Fertilized seeds, suspended in milk.
Let's find out how that happens.
Six long stamens hold pollen-filled anthers,
designed to catch wind and attract pollinators.
When the reproductive organs are touched lightly,
the pollen grain lands on a stigma and grows a tube
down through the style,
secreting enzymes to digest a pathway.
Nectar, scent, secret sticky parts.
Three spotted petals flutter.

The crane need not show itself
on a high hill.
Its young will hear its note,
recognize, and give answer.

Songs of the Departing

I tell all my "I was alive when . . ." stories.
The young people at the *seder* table look quickly at each other,
meaning, Let's go to the bedroom.

My parents talked about Sinatra
and Dorsey playing Revere Beach,
and not enough food.

My grandparents bickered and whispered in Yiddish.
My sister and I would leave the table
to sing Dowland madrigals in the den.
Weep no more, sad fountains.

Tonight, we open the door to Elijah the Prophet,
an old beggar, who will bring the Messiah
speedily, in our time.

Open the door so I can walk outside
and burn my memories
for some heat.

L.A. Chess Club

The man would say, "Mate in five," or "Mate in twelve,"
or he'd just crush me without a word.
I was a boy.
It was horrible, parts of me hacked off, movement confined,
pawns falling one by one.
I remember how my options closed down, but not his name.
He was small, with thin fingers
that rushed the pieces,
whacked them down, then removed mine with a flourish
and a chuckle.
(Did I want to lose,
so I wouldn't risk disappointing him?)
I only know that I kept quiet, letting it happen,
beginning to see many moves ahead.
This thing going, that thing useless,
the other thing not powerful enough
to make up for the losses,
his and mine.

Alchemy

You are mercury; I am sulfur.
I, silver; you, leaves.
You, aqua regia; I, soil.
I can't code-switch to your language,
which is the sum of generations in your mouth.
You do not switch to my Yiddish-inflected lament,
"Oy, Master of the Universe,
why have you let the Russians rule us again?"
Still, you and I are a *coniunctio oppositorum*.
Red vermillion; black iron-gall ink.
Our words meld in the alembic of this art,
even if we are each indissoluble.

Pebble

A sea-rounded quartz pebble from a cow field—
spiny spurge and thistle sprouting from clay,
fifty miles inland.
Child-tossed? Bird-beak-carried?

I walked across the difficult pasture,
pocked with deep cattle-foot holes.
Saw many randomly strewn sea stones amid cow patties.
How did they get there?

Hiked uphill to a ridge overlooking the next valley.
Reached a spine of rocks, worn, lichen-splotched,
half-buried in spring-green grass and orange poppies.
This broken spine, soft sandstone
cementing harder, ocean-smoothed pebbles
into rough, eroding terrazzo, out of which fell the sea stones,
later to be washed by rains
and sprinkled into the valleys on either side.

I brought the pebble home to a table near a window.
I feel its ochre skin, which is the texture of my skin, but hard as topaz.
It is where art lives, and I can rub it in my palms.

What We Found During Quarantine

My wife, with her tiny Fiskars scissors,
bends over the neighbors' plant beds and cuts.
I stand guard, signaling "Enough"
with my right palm, before she's done.
I stuff orange mini-roses and sky-blue cornflowers
into my puffing shirt and jacket.
Scarecrow with blossoms sticking out every evening.
In danger, we become quiet conspirators, all gesture.
For these times, we aren't bickering.

My wife arranges them in little vases on the bookshelf,
each day adding and weeding.
Today, it's caterpillar phacelia, nigella, pea,
snakeroot, rose, vervain, coralroot.
Tomorrow, maybe poppy or bearded iris.
I photograph the array every morning,
documenting time.

We stayed who we had become, together.
A couple stealing flowers.

Reconciling Behind the Barn

I sit alone on a cinder block. It is cold.
The great clouds taller than mountains.
Alone fills the meadow. Fills the woods.
Fills the maples and aspens. And me.
There are gouges in the meadow
where Johnson dragged the trees he logged.
Sometimes I cannot tell what is missing.
I sit on the cold cinder block,
and all around me brown mushrooms are curling.

The Woman in the Tree

Crazy up there doing everything on her platform,
alone. It's hardest for her at dusk, I imagine.
Because the meadow stretches away like the sea
into sadness. And the little lights of houses
blink on. She's making it all up for herself,
and the things she's inventing make it impossible
for her down here. She slips into the cool air.
Eats grisettes and moss. Hums to herself.
Watches after-storm clouds. Loneliness
hammering her into something new.

The Voices in the Trees

When they're lonely, Tree Sitters hoot
    down to Ground Sitters, in their filthy camp,
who hoot back at dusk through the forest.
      After two years of Tree Sit, the University
is crazy with anger. Extractors move in
    with cherry pickers. Begin to cut food bags
out of a Deodar Cedar with polepruners, polesaws,
    chainsaws. Target the traverse lines
that Sitters use to move smoothly from tree to tree.
    Then cut safety lines and sleeping platforms.
Extractors chase Sitters, limb to limb.
    Crane-man swings his wrecking-ball hook
at Dumpster Muffin in the big redwood.
    Extractor threatens Fresh's stomach with a hook knife.
Millipede kicks Extractor's balls before he grabs
    and hog-ties her. One girl flinches and falls.
Sitters throw stored shit at a basket of Extractors
    being lowered into an oak. I hear wind. I hear sobbing.
Hear prayers for Mother Earth. Hear pride.
    Hear Frederick Law Olmstead praising the grove he made.
I hear Gerard Manley Hopkins lamenting the Binsey Poplars they cut.
    I hear pulp ground to powder. I hear branches obliterated
in crushers. Shrubs flattened.
    Sitters lose the battle.
Extractors fail to snip out the children's tongues.

Tree Sitters

One teenager bites another.   The point is to invade
and infect the newcomer.   Wildness enters him,
spreading disturbance,   packing wolves into his arms.
They pierce their tongues   and scavenge dumpsters.
They go up into trees.   Smoke weed and burn sage.
A small tribe that moves   quietly and swiftly
through the canopy,   shaking leaves lightly,
evading police   and the other powers.
Body lice don't matter   because they're already
in paradise.   My son is one of them,
with his forest name, Chanterelle.   I pass his sacred grove every day
and often see him lounging   in the oaks with his friends,
Millipede, Fresh, Compost, Citizen, Creek.
I imagine they're saying   how crazy the adults are,
down there in a failing civilization.   And how relieved
they feel in their smoky tree-village,   waiting in the leaves,
calm and watchful, almost invisible.   When I'm closest
to his platform, I whistle for my boy   in the old way,
when he would run into my hands.   He always whistles back,
the little Indian trick we share.   Two birds whistling
We are still here.

Antigone

For the Berkeley Tree Sitters, 2006–2008

Antigone is played by two girls, Millipede
    and Dumpster Muffin. Creon, by the Chancellor
of the University. He must protect the institution
    against the girls. The forty-two trees to be cut down
to make space for a state-of-the-art athletic facility
    are Antigone's rebel brother, Polyneices, dead in a field,
unburied on Creon's order. "Who will wash his body?"
    the girls plead. "Who will sing for him?"
The girls will sit in trees until the Chancellor gives in.
    The Antigones are crazy. Creon will win.
The trees will be hacked down and fed into a chipper.
    We will know it is art because Creon will try
to break the Antigones as hard as he can,
    but they will not break. The Chancellor will give parties
for donors. The Chorus of Filthy Kids will invade
    the parties, screaming that Creon violated the grove.
He will probably live long and prosper anyway.
    After prison, the girls will find more trees to sit in,
maybe even growing old this way. They will weep
    often for the trees they remember. The Furies will stir,
sometimes incinerating a king, but mostly just going
    back to sleep. The girls will make something durable
and beautiful because they were strong and did not break.

The Oak Grove on Piedmont Way
Slated for Extirpation by the University

The grove's only voice is wind,
a chorus of soft lisps.
A tree cannot persuade,
so weak it is and helpless
against argument and money.
A tree's effect is like music
without words. Spreading
out from a still center
then blooming into time,
shapes, exultation, grief,
and the many orders of green.
The only way for a tree
to prevail is for a human to yield
completely to it.
The way I might sometimes permit
music to enter me. Perhaps when I'm tired,
sick, or defenseless.
Then sound is suspended
until a silence glows around it,
and at once I shake
for holding so much.
Phrases, movements, skies
winds, meadows.
The oaks applying their thousand
subtle fingers to peel me.

The Man Gives Up Lying
After Meeting the *Dybbuk*

The man is a calf crumpling
on thin legs. His sorrows rise.
"Why don't you just take what you *want?*"
A petal opens. A thousand more.
The man cannot hide.
He's kissing his son's hair now.
Waking him slowly. The boy grumpy.
The man whispers,
"Let's start with breakfast.
Tell me what you want for breakfast."

Shadows

The summer heat is thick today; vapors rise from watered grass.

This heat is not the thin clear kind that makes a mountain seem closer.

I'm walking to my bench under the sycamore in a corner of the park.

A group of crows already occupies the shadow.

They whoosh off, taking parts of the shadow with them.

Two skinny squirrels undulate across the lawn. Stop.

Dig for food. The male quickly mounts the female,

hops off, then chases her up the sycamore tree.

The summer kids are screaming in the distant pool.

A blue garbage truck rumbles and screeches by the picnic area.

A flock of gnatcatchers *tsp-tsp-tsp* in an oleander bush.

The sycamore tree expands and contracts smoothly in the hot wind.

Finally the heat is too much for me.

I get up from my bench and walk out under the trees,

shadow by shadow.

Mount Diablo

I'm alone on its sun-blasted north face,
amid patchy, charred sandstone.
Knobs of weathered green rock.
Plugs of basalt. Dikes of pillow lava.
Blueschist, shale, serpentine, graywacke.
Heat-cracked knuckles of chert.

Without these eyes, how could I be calmed by rocks?
Without this skin, how could I be laved
in an ocean of blue oaks and junipers?
How would I be washed in a swaying sea of pines?
Without these perishing senses, how could I feel time
in the long, muffled exhalations of lobed oaks?
Without a hand, how could I hold
the smooth muscle of a manzanita?
Without this old body
how could I walk off the path into Hallelujah?

Paradise Without Illusion

Jack is napping in the garden
of Sunrise Skilled Nursing.
I am half-napping next to him.
We're facing into the early spring
breeze, two old leathery Jews
on a beach in Florida. Clouds pass,
light and shade fall on our eyes,
and the sun stings our cheeks.
It's a quiet voyage we're on.
A string quartet is being piped in.
Nurses and attendants assume
I'm Jack's son. When they ask,
I tell them I am, which is true enough.
Jack hears everything.
Sometimes I catch a slit of blue eye.
Sometimes he nods "Yes" or "No."
Sometimes he reaches to me
with his long fingers.

Making a Run for It

Jack said maybe he'd like to go to Paros to die.
A house on the mountain might be too hard,
he agrees, but something in town would be nice.
Today Jack is arguing in the old way,
lamenting that the bad people have won.
Today I tell him I almost think he could do it.
Three days on the plane with a nurse,
one night in Piraeus, a slow ferry to the island,
and finally the new place and Albanian caregivers.
Jack half-smiles, meaning it will never happen,
it is finished, it is too late to climb the steps.
But he tells me that I should go somewhere.
I can't have my life here, around the comfortable people.
Am I getting too scared, I ask myself, to go all the way?
Jack fell last week, pushing himself out
of his wheelchair, trying to get to the fish tank.

Brief for Reality

I'm nearly dead, he says, as we walk
around the Marina for a little clean sea air.
Everything besides himself seems so alive, he says.
Me, joking about women. A fat man spraying
a boat with water. The ground squirrels
coming up to us, with their liquid black eyes,
insisting on anything to eat. Jack is exhausted
from the short shuffle along the beach,
but I'm not convinced he's as dead as he says.
Yes, so much has been eaten away. "My life,"
he says, "is disappearing." Jack's intense sweetness
is different these days than his sweetness mixed
with sudden fierceness when he was younger.
Yes, now it's helpless sweetness. But when I remark
on the beauty of the view, he resists. "I want the other."

The Old Man Asks
What Is Beyond Contentment

"What is the tone of your life?"

"Tone, Jack?"

He puts together more words than I've heard from him in weeks.

"Desperate, deep, fearful, courageous?"

"Yes, Jack, all of them."

"That's good," he says, and asks, "What is the shape of your life?"

"Shape, Jack?"

"Drifting, incidental, purposeful, flowing?"

He asks, again, "What is your life's tone, your life's shape?"

I answer more carefully.

I have power, depth, fear

as my tones, and uncertainty as my shape.

"I was frightened," he says, "that you would just float:

What do you want to do with the rest of your life?"

Which he asks of everyone in the assisted living facility.

He thinks all the residents hate him.

I tell him how the way he asks questions,

over and over, until an answer begins to clarify

as I stutter and sound stupid trying to make sense

out of myself inside his bewildering

assignments, has changed me

as he twists himself and me into odd angles.

His tone is will. His shape is helpless.

The rest of his life is grief.

Selfish

Death is natural. We live and then we die.
Not something to have a service about, with music,
photos of the departed, and long speeches.
Just the fact, swiftly told. The way Hindu men
run with the corpse lit by sparking torches.
At my age, it's essential not to read the paper.
Letting the world go on without me.
Being at the edge, in an eddy, a tiny, shriveled planet.
I like sitting on the stone wall of the Catskills
with a hat on my head, not moving.
The sun does the moving. I don't like groups either,
the fuss they are always making about this one
and that one and what she thinks and how he
is belittling the other one. And visiting Jack
is getting harder as it all grows uglier.
His dementia, me having to feed him by hand,
breaking off pieces of the lemon bar and putting them
into his mostly toothless mouth, eating being his great
pleasure. And then him falling asleep and drooling
as we're sitting in the garden, which is not at all peaceful
with the TVs blasting from the adjacent rooms.
No, I know that Jack does not want me to visit by guilt,
but would relish my being alone on a rock wall.
People phone me, they want help and company,
they want not to be alone. I'm sorry,
I think for a second, before I don't pick up.

Alzheimer's Wing

I used to think it was charming the way Jack
would forget the name of a famous poet.
(Maybe he was slyly commenting on their skill.)
He'd give me clues, a few words, an image,
a city, and I'd guess. I loved to pretend to be lost
with him in the tangled alleys of Paros. I thought
he thought we both enjoyed the wandering
and laughing, amid cats spurting out of trash cans.
I imitated Jack at the market when he'd hold out
his palm full of Euros and the young Greek cashier
would smile and take the right money.

Show Don't Tell

He can't find his words.
The greatest living American
poet unable to say "pencil"
when the doctor holds it up.
Or "light" when she tips
the lamp. Or the name
of the new president.
After puzzling for a while,
he finally whispers, It is what
I write poems with.
It is what illuminates
the room. It is the better man,
who came after Bush. Function
he describes, but not its name.
When the doctor asks him to name a fork,
he brings it trembling to his lips.

It Is Finished

The hour today was quiet. Not sad
but thoughtful. Jack looked at me
hard blue through half-closed lids.
"It is finished." I did not argue.
Because it was true. I saw he'd lost
more teeth and could only nap
to keep some measure of silence
amid the din of his nursing home.
My feelings were my words.
I looked steadily back at him
in silence. We die alone.

Jack's Terror in Assisted Living

My world is so tiny.
This room, some TV,
a walk to the food.
The others also have tiny
worlds that don't touch
anybody else's.
I see in the others
my own death.
A woman visited me.
She said she had been important,
that we had something passionate.
I couldn't remember anything.
All I could do was be nice.
It was frightening.
And you, this man I love.
I am ashamed.
Sometimes I don't know
your name.
I worry what will happen next.
My life is disappearing.
Will you wall me out?
Write your name here
so I will know you that way.
When will you be back?
When will you be back?
When will you be back?

Having What He Has

Jack can't walk anymore. Takes tiny
shuffling steps. I keep having to say,
"Jack, one foot, then the other,"
over and over to make progress
toward dining room or porch.
He looked up at me this morning
and said "Please, no more stories
of my old life; I've forgotten it."
His blue eyes steady and open,
left lid drooping a little.
"I want to live this life now,
the truth." We walk to the courtyard
to find some rosemary
and lavender to crush.

Losing What He Has

I don't know where I am at night, Jack says.
Who are the people I trust.
Their stories, and how I fit.
How they will find me
when I'm lost and helpless.
I don't remember my homes.
Or the bad years, or the good.
What day, week, time
it is. What my penis did.
I know I have death left.
You can't imagine
how strange it is
to see my death so visible
in these old people
in the dining room.
Eating whatever is put
in front of us by kind aides.
You can't imagine my grief.
That these are the last
things I will do.

Wanting What He Lost

Jack was young when I met him. Today he is old.
I go to his room every day to let him see my face,
so he'll have that small, regular thing, smiling.
This afternoon, I'm trimming his beard on the sunny patio.
Because, he says, he doesn't want Linda to see the ugliness
when she comes on Tuesday. The long hairs fall
on his sweater. Later I brush it off, and it flies.
He's happy, and I'm happy. A barber and his man.
No one, I think, will twitter or facebook or cell phone
or talk politics or new science or the illusion of free will,
when they are old and butchered by God, who took
the ears from Beethoven and the memory from Jack.
At the end of their life and history, people want meaning
and safety, and to believe they really did choose love.
They want to wake up from a sleep of long dreams.
And then swim, maybe. Or at least remember
the way they were fully passionate those few times.
They want the pleasure of washing their shirt.
Going on a walk. And meeting friends of many years.
To gaze at their faces, touch their shoulder.
Feel the tug of the golden thread between them.

His Changing Relationship
with the World at Eighty-Five

Jack would like to try to write a poem.
His eyes don't see, his hands don't connect
to his brain, his mouth and mind don't talk.
But many days Jack laughs and claps his hands
silently when we talk about our friends.
Many days Jack forces himself out of bed
when I'm leaving so he can stand there,
watching me as far as the walls permit,
the way he used to stand on the quiet street
watching my car disappear. Watching,
to let me know his care extended all that way,
and through the time of my going down
the leafy summer afternoon. I've seen Jack's poems.
They are red, unreadable, and go around the edges
of the paper. Even Jack can't tell what's there,
except that it's about losing everything.
Maybe, I tell him, I can type them up.
Meanwhile, we walk arm in arm
outside to the patio where sadness enters him.
Does he still have his money? Can he write anymore?
Where are his friends? Why has life changed?
I wonder if change always means breakdown,
or if it includes triumph, if only briefly,
the two alternating, but us not knowing
which one will be ascendant until the very end.

Still Making a Disturbance

I think he's trying to tell me something
about himself, stuck here in assisted living,
when he says it's not bad, but it's hard
for him to know what's surprising.
Yes, I think, his disappearing mind
and shrinking body in the routines
of food, TV, sleep, shuffling around.
He bends toward me so our foreheads
touch, and his eyes are watching mine.
Says he thinks I've gotten content.
Accepting only the nice kind of life.
Nobody excited. Just drifting.
Nothing special. No larger dreams.
Mild and pleasant. Jack is looking
hard at me. You must be fierce, he says.
Because soon you're going to be old.
I want something more deep for you.
Strong. Lovely. With power.
With yearning for something that matters.
Time is running out, and you are just
enjoying a meanwhile life. Ask yourself
what is beyond contentment.

Gratitude

I hear a thud the size of a crow.
It is Jack falling in the hallway.
Then a trip to emergency and stitches.
He can't talk about what happened.
Because dementia continually shoves clay
down his throat. Shadows of forests
and cities flicker and hiss in his brain's
walnut corpse. Alzheimer's pounds
his delight, hammers it into a sheet,
tears it to pieces, then vacuums it
away. One glistening half-memory
sticks to the floor. A fleck
of Jack's native pleasure twitches
in the last currents he will feel.
But even sorrow has its limit.
He opens his mouth like a bird's
when I hold up a spoonful of chocolate cake.

Meetings with Jack

He stares at me, a force-field of slowness.
When I leave his house, I see,
in my rear-view mirror, him watching my car
go down the maple-canopied road
until I turn and his white face disappears.
I've never known time like his.
Each teacup, each step, each word
given ample space to flare into its own clarity.
He thinks at the speed of walking.
Only months before— in his slow dying of Alzheimer's—
he still had the presence of mind to say
he wanted to know precisely
what dying was. No anodynes.
Time in which to expand into the farthest cells.
Even now, he is able to write messages to himself in faint pencil
on the backs of boxes, random pages of books, scraps of paper.
He hides them from himself.
So that he might find them by accident.
After Jack died, I helped clean out his room:
Muscle. Death. Luck. Take your place. Stand on the ground.

Zoo

The old lady volunteers once a month to oil the tortoise.
He's over a hundred-twenty years old.
I think he must like the grooming
because he stays still while she rubs him with soaked rags.
She tells me he can feel her vibrations because his spine
is right against the shell. The tortoise stretches out
his neck and drays his three-hundred pound land-mass
on elephant-like feet. He's looking at me.
Open. Blink. Open. Sniffing the air
with two nostril-holes. I ask if he has personality.
"Yes," the old lady says, "he's patient and interested.
He's got everything he needs. House on his back.
Too slow to get perturbed,
unlike the quick fruit bats who pick
and tease with their long, thin hands and chase
each other upside down across the roost."
I guess that the tortoise can't get at anyone before his anger
runs out. And who can get at him, a sensitive rock?
A stone in the creek, water splashing all over it,
while fish, birds, and insects whip around.
I see that he watches the zoo goers watching him.
He could do that for a decade, looking at the tiny hairs
on one child's cheek change into whiskers.
But the people always go before he is finished.

Field Trip to the Blacksmith Shop

The children line up behind the anvil,
big goggles on their heads. The smith
puts down hot red metal for beating
and the smooth uncanny bending, after.
Heat is pushing hard into their cherry faces.
I'm watching how my son takes to this changing
one thing into a different thing.
How he, in his slim boy's body, loves
sparks spraying from coal. Something
beginning for him, here at nine.
I know it by the way he studies
his Transformers, tongue
between his lips. The Dinobot
swiveling from assault vehicle to robot
to beast. The boy loving the tricks
embedded there. Preferring this work
to supper or talking to me.
Bringing something new out of the last
thing. Perishing again in the furnace
of his body. The way God made *Abraham*
out of a little goatherd. How after
the iron is dug out it can be hammered
into figs or knives. How the black
crust cracks off the glowing bud.

Sayings of the Father

At five years old I learned Bible Stories.
At ten, I began Mishnah.
At thirteen, found my penis.
At fourteen, I rejected God for fossils of spiral turritella shells.
At fifteen, Shakespeare stripped my mind naked,
and at eighteen, the Greeks penetrated my tendons.
I could feel them in my arms.
At twenty-one, I found pursuit. Thirty, power.
Forty, I glimpsed they were not enough.
Sixty-six-and-three-months, I ruptured two discs.
At sixty-seven, I came to believe that I might use a word like "true"
and then risk everything to mean it.
Sixty-seven-and-four-months, I discovered I was invisible,
as the Talmud taught, so I began to understand
I might be only background to the world of people.
Now, at seventy-two, I begin to ask myself, Is my life a success?
Two months ago I went into my back yard, and planted seeds
of the wildflower *Nemophela menziesii*.
This morning I found their sky-blue cups.

Temenos

I only take the fruiting bodies—for beauty and taste—
sometimes even for the excitement of their liver-eating
and mind-splitting.
I pick life, for life. I learn shapes of life, for life.
I pick them to teach my son who, because he is new
and low to the ground,
teaches me how to find them.

"No Mushroom Picking!"—underneath a skull.
Signage at the trailhead.

A park ranger sets up the low, electric fence of his attention,
under which we must pass, limbo-like.
He will try to discern our true intentions:
"What are you doing here today?" he asks, looking at our backpacks.
"Enjoying the contorted pines, pygmy cypresses,
rare acidic hard-pan, and the rough weather," I half-lie. "OK, pass."
(I half-worry that I've taught my son how to lie
in order to steal.)

Deep into the forest, we scan the duff for humps
and the small diagnostic slits of white, amid brown needles:
Matsutake.
My boy shows me how to find their dwelling places
by disappearing into the their clean, perfumed flesh.

Reincarnation

The man is half-alive in his own tomb
watching TV. A tomb constructed
of marble made of the light
he had hidden since he was a boy.
The angel pushes the tomb door open,
crackling with dry ivy and dust.
She holds a torch.
Revealing the man to himself,
sitting there, stalled between lives.
Resurrection, she says, is not from man to swan,
man to squirrel, man to saint, man to farmer.
It is man to himself, new and original.
Ancient and uncovered.
Which takes a death to keep it going.

Facing It

There are few people on the mountain today.
One is a South Asian man (we recognize each other
in our solitude, and we pass respectfully in silence).
There is a Russian-speaking couple.
Their cheeks are so red—as though the sun has gotten inside them.
The quiet here is desert-like.
No planes in the sky, all grounded due to smoke.
I hear a background tone inside me:
the cosmos has arrived in my head.
An afternoon wind suddenly cleans the sky, light floods in.
The leaves of every sage plant curl up to protect
the slender threads of moisture inside.
I take a trail though generously spaced blue oaks,
columns rising out of blond oats.
None of the people I've seen have come this far
into the colossal wreck of Mount Diablo.
I only *think* I've escaped. To the east, a continent looms.

Snakes

My son and I chance upon a rattlesnake baby
stretched out to take in cool afternoon shadows and wind.
Here is the perfection of indifference.
Wedge-head, tiny rattle, blotches of buff, bronze, gold, ochre.
Ben, our Navajo friend, throws corn pollen
in the eyes of snakes he encounters, and chants.
This enrages a snake, he tells us.
He is afraid because they are an earthly manifestation
of Lightning People, in turn related to the Thunders.
Ben insists we must remember our thoughts
at the moment of seeing a snake.
I'm thinking about the wild turkeys we saw
prowling and pacing, kick-scratching the duff for seeds.
Quiet eaters in the shade. A tribe descended from reptiles.
Iridescent feathers and ugly, floppy necks.
I'm also thinking about the faded purple of a coyote mint blossom
and how I didn't have enough money this month.
As our snake starts to move off slowly into wild oats,
I am thinking, here with my son, how lucky I am.
We walk into the folds of a mountain,
come to the Omphalos of a New World.
Small rock pool, decorated with hanging crimson lanterns,
yellow columbines, twisted dwarf junipers, dried stalks of grasses,
star-burst umbels, and spent lilies—which I can pretend
are doing their best to tremble toward us.

Moorchild

This boy was alone every lunch.
He heard the kids on the hot playground
playing dodge ball, tether ball, foursquare, chase.
Crawled through a hole in the fence, down
into the gully's wet throat to the willows and walnuts,
where he drank the creek's amber odors.
Did the teachers see him disappear, light as a seed
and beyond time as the bells rang?
Why did he start?
No one saw and no one worried.
Green breath rose to him from ferns,
sycamores extended their palms.
Flycatchers and gnatcatchers
were *cherubim* in the oaks. Were *seraphim*
on the sandstone. Were *malachim* in the wind.
On his this shoulders,
glowing capes of moss.

Nomenclature

The bird was hidden in a bog, about 2000 feet,
at an alien rainforest margin on Maui.
The bird's calls:
uuuuuuuuuuuuuuuuuuuuuuuuuuuuuu-guisu
A long, steady whistle, followed by a short trill;
then a long, steady whistle, about a fourth above the first,
followed by a short trill; then another long, clear whistle
about seven steps below the last, and the trill.
I whistle-talked with the bird for twenty minutes.
I tried to key out the bird from a book.
Finally wrote Professor VanderWerf,
who answered immediately: Bush warbler.
Native to Japan, introduced to Hawaii
decades ago, now widespread in forests.
You rarely see the bird: tiny, drab, secretive,
with pale eyebrows. The Japanese name is *Uguisu*,
an onomatopoeia for its song.
It means plums blossoming in early spring.

What Makes Sense

I'm sick of crap with humans who keep each other at a distance.
Farther than two inches away, humans are impossible to each other.
Within two inches, they are also impossible, but are entangled,
sometimes for the good.
What makes sense is when humans talk to each other in parks.
Then it's about babies, pets, the squirrels, the smell of cooking meats,
what they did when they were working, how is their health.
Maybe they even tell each other something true
that they couldn't tell to one of the two-inches-away people.
What makes sense is a terrestrial umbel of purple stars—cluster lilies—
detonating amid the tawny grasses of summer.
I'm sick of news and politics.
What makes sense is a grove of conifers bathing me in volatile elements.
What makes sense is to walk away from it all and into my sole body
as it struggles up a sandstone slope chock full of Miocene clamshells.
At the top, I see the many greens of a meadow
that somehow survived the apocalypse.
The important question now is, What can I do with these greens?

Measuring the Kingdom

My son and I meet a young woman on the trail. She's holding a clip-
board and writing on graph paper. "I'm mapping the geology
of the area." The seam of sandstone we're standing on, she tells us,
was an Eocene beach. Under pressure for twenty million years
it became stone, later uplifted and made visible.
"Tablets of the Interior," we joke.
I think: the smooth caves blown into the rock's soft flanks
are sepulchers of seas. The seam of coal across the canyon, she says,
was a richly vegetated freshwater marsh, with rotting algae, reeds,
horsetails, willows, eel grass, ferns.
Buried in silt and squeezed in the Carboniferous Period,
it became peat, then lignite, finally coal. It too was uplifted:
"Darkness Visible," I think. My son and I have come to this canyon
since he was a toddler, twenty-five years ago. Today, we have a guest
teaching us the natural history of the outcrop
from which my son will throw my ashes and dust.
We're standing on some mine tailings, a few decayed stumps
of a huge crusher that went silent a century ago. The noise
must have been terrific. Shadows of cliff swallows cross our eyes.
Five sheep chew softly.

Encounter

The newt is velvety burnt umber with an orange belly
and small, fine hands. She treads on leaf-litter
toward any puddle or pool.
She has neither skin-toxins nor speed,
only the color of autumn leaves.
She crawls onto the back of my hand, tickling.
I turn from solid to liquid.

Hawk

I feel air-beats before I see her.
Then wings, as she hovers before me.
Fanned rusty tail, shining topaz eyes.
I reach out my arm, *half*-hoping.
Her talons grip the tendons of my hand.
They do not break the skin,
but hold me between pierce and loose.
After I calm, she allows me to touch her neck.
I say a final goodbye to my parents.

Walk #3428

Lit up my Habana Torpedo in the windshadow
of a building. Talked to a smoking, overweight,
unhealthy-looking lawyer (whose name I've never known)
about the death of his dog. Walked along in the light
and shadow that sycamores make in the afternoon.
Was finally hailed by a crazy-looking
300-pound man reading exercise books on the patio
of a Barnes & Noble café. I could see him surprised
when I actually came over (surprising myself) and sat down.
He handed me a chart of calories burned for various
activities per pound of body weight per hour.
Of interest to both of us was that digging and hoeing
equaled waterskiing, at 3.2 calories burned.
He asked me to do the math because his mind
had been ruined by drugs. I calculated for Joe
that he'd burn 920 calories in his mother's garden.
He was happy. I left him, continued my walk,
burning 2.4 calories, and stopped at an art gallery
showing Old-Master-style portraits of animals
running, lunging, eating, rutting, lumbering.
While their own skulls floated above each.

Perspective

The world of the permanent park-dwellers goes on, uninterested
in Washington D.C, or even in the Concord City Council.
Specimen trees from around the world have made their peace
with local Delta winds and clay soil.
Italian stone pine, New England paper birch, eastern white oak,
red cedar, tulip tree, ash, beech, Sitka spruce, western sycamore,
redwood, California live oak. And the great mycelial net
pleaching diverse trees' rootlets across thirty acres of parkland.
Also uninterested in human politics are the creatures
who make their livings here: squirrel, crow, worm, vole, sparrow, robin.
Except that some do like the peanuts the lonely man, Max, tosses.
Max, the retired PG&E high lineman, tells me he has a titanium knee
and skull. Tells me how he broke up with his girlfriend
because she got fat during the pandemic.
Now his dog's tumor is so big that her belly drags on the grass.
The dog that used to be so fast she caught five squirrels.
We humans come and go. Trees abide.
Small lives of the field run and die. Soil abides.
My anger, care, worry, illness— absolutely irrelevant to grass.
A wind picks up in the afternoon:
the product of hot rising air in the Great Central Valley
and of cold sea air rushing into the void.

Spit into Wind

The man uses a leaf-blower daily, strapped to his back, in hot sun,
in windstorm, in rain.
The man walks around the block every day from Point A to Point A,
which on some days is impossible to find.
"Stop chasing squirrels and sniffing that other dog's ass!" the man yells
at his dog who died three years ago today.
The man won't drink wine, but will eat garlic during plague,
won't watch TV, but will read a book, tearing out each page
as he finishes it.
The man has ended a relationship with god,
or the god he once thought was god,
and was really the iron fence at the end of the block.
Today the man's hands have grown too long for masturbating,
yesterday they were too short.
The man tries to kill off an entire ants' nest under his grapefruit tree
with one swipe of his shovel. His shoulder will never be the same.

The Electrical Flow in My Body Unblocks

Weedlot I've kept my eye on for thirty years.
Profusion of rank plants, prickly lettuce, neglected mallow,
hawkweed, common to urban wastes.
Rats, run-hugging retaining walls.
Stubborn weedlot: a shining green pelt amid dense city blocks.
Stubbornness it teaches me.
I make love to my wife, even if all around us
circuits are burning.
I remember a viper I stepped on at midnight
in the Anza-Borrego Badlands. It reared to strike.
How I scream-danced
until it slid away into a crack.
Cactus needles piercing the milky way
in the warm windy sky.

Raze or Rest

Bud or rot; finger or cloud; bird or rock;
hawk or trout; diamond or lead; wind or ice;
sunlight or inner pith; flute-sound or coffin; dance or die.
This or that, people insist. *Good or bad.*
Cantons of your blood revolt.
You know the trembling inside happiness.
The happiness inside catastrophe.
You know how wind translates force
into the soughing of maples.
You want the third thing always:
that which you whisper between a star
and the dirt.
How long it took you to find
your own simple form.
You walk in the silence of Coldwater Canyon.

The Persistence of Nothing

When we are old enough to go to funerals regularly,
and when we get up earlier than most households
to witness the eddies of fresh air
and the thin simple bird-whistles at dawn,
and when the quiet inside exchanges with the quiet outside
for a few minutes of equilibrium,
then we can imagine our extinction.
We are not solid, even for our children.
Just collections of thought, memory, bad guesses.
All of us a feeble architecture, assembling and collapsing.
We are also like the plaster of a Roman ruin.
Colors seep through, and we can make out peacocks and figs.
Young girls dancing on flowering grasses
and the mystery of lyres we cannot hear.
Adonis dead, held by his Venus,
and turned into something like stars or words by our Ovid.
A shower of molecules over the immense, blinding sea.

Squirrels

The man carries his boy on his shoulders.
The boy laughs and pats the man's head.
Father and son are travelers beneath a windy sixty feet
of many-voiced hardwoods.
Safe inside the deep luxury of green.
They reach a flat blue slate rock floating above a spring.
Time for lunch. Tuna fish and carrot sticks.
As they eat, they watch two squirrels chewing beechnuts.
The boy is happy everybody is eating together.
Now he's asking his father questions about squirrels—
their food, homes, babies, lifespan, language.
What do the *chuff-chuffs* mean?
Can squirrels tell jokes?
The man is making up answers, surfing the waves
of his child's mind, which, the man thinks,
is a mind of a different species.
Lucky the boy brings him along.

Waiting for the Third Thing

Alejandro the Bather comes every other day to wash my friend Bill.

The Bather is expert at cleaning without moving his man from a bed.

Hair, beard, hands, legs, groin, feet.

The Bather even changes the shit-clogged colostomy bag, smiling.

He folds and unfolds the sheets, origami-style.

Pleasure settles across my friend's face.

He takes a sip of pomegranate juice.

We listen to the Lark Ascending of Vaughan Williams.

My friend weeps quietly, eyes turned away.

He does not want to leave.

The sun moves over him.

Climate

My son and I see the change.
Since he was a toddler (him straddling my shoulders,
patting my head), we've hiked to our secret, personal spot.
Chanterelles used to fruit there for us—
fat, flushed, abundant in September.
Now, a few push up skinny in December—it's a lucky year.
Juniper Spring, which feeds its own perennial creek,
has shrunk to a damp stain.
We used to see ladybugs massed for warmth in winter on mossy rocks,
heard bird-rackets at dawn, throngs of bees zipping
in and out of the hollow oak.

Now, the laurels are empty at dusk.
Now, summer burns forward and back in time from the middle.
The yellow, tubular, lobe-mouthed muskflowers
we used to find by odor alone, scent the air no more.

And yet—orange lichen on scorched chert,
rattlesnakes, wolf spiders, vultures, crows, rats,
spiny cocklebur, thistle, pigweed, creosote.
My son and I note their persistence.

Two in the Park

The Queen of Evening steals light from the maples.
The Sorcerer of Wind pierces me, I leak into dusk.
The Sword of Spades taps my spine into flame.
The Lord of Beaks stabs my eye into spray.
The King of Leaves slices my heart to lace.
A woman is bathing in the fountain at dusk.
Singing to herself. We are so different
that we can't misunderstand each other.

Gridley Springs

I've followed last summer's wildfire to hunt for fire-followers.
I haven't seen them in fifty years.
I bend to smell a big, blue cup of *Phacelia grandiflora*.
Then find a yellow chalice of *Calochortus clavatus*
amid scorched sandstone.
Then a cardinal-colored catchfly, a purple-knobbed holy-herb,
a Lindley's blazing star, a hot-rock live-forever.
I hear myself, *One more time; one more spring*.
And afterward, on the road out,
I eat two warm, dripping oranges
stolen from a grove still yielding.

Disappearance

The antlion waits hidden at the bottom of the tiny pit of sand
which it engineered at a deadly angle for unlucky ants.
Once an ant crosses the crater rim, it cannot struggle out,
its furious leg-work only ensuring that it slides back,
deeper and deeper, as it tires, toward the antlion's grip and maw.
The whole ant-cohort is being finished off this way, one after
another—the shy, the bold, the forager, the fighter, the builder.

Chant for the End of Time

hespero, hespero, hespero,
zephyros, zephyros,
winds of the west,
zephyros, zephyros,
Hesperus,
hesperolinon,
hesperolinon,
flax of the west,
eosphorus, cephalus,
spiritus, hesperos,
boreas, hesperos,
flax of the west,
phosphorus, eos,
suther, suther,
vesper, Lucifer.
Te ta. **Te** ta. **Te** ta.

Last Things Created on the Eve of the First Sabbath

Mouth of the earth, punched into the sandstone cliff behind my house.
Mouth of a spring, gushing from Banias cave
at the foot of Mount Hermon. Mouth of the well,
amid maples and birch of Boscu's farm.
The piled stone walls around his meadows.
Chewing mouth of the donkey, standing on three legs,
summer hay reaching up to its fetlocks. A rainbow.
Scrambled eggs my grandmother fed me in her yellow kitchen.
The temples of imagination crafted from a substance
that cuts through iron, stone, diamond.
The story I wrote of how I'd sneak into the bathroom on Sabbath Eve,
rub on the Old Spice After Shave, then return to table,
believing that no one could tell.
And Mrs. Stanley's note to me: "You can be a poet."
Some people say also demons were created on that eve,
the grave of Moses, the Ram of Abraham,
and tongs to lift out of the iron blast furnace a boy.

Worth, Measured As

The wooden benches in the old parts of American towns
were built for sitting comfortably. For the man on the bench,
a cigar was the measure of time,
steadily burning its folds of leaves into ringlets of air.
Hand-played music unfurls into a sculpture of time.
Reading a mind layered into a Bach score is a slow labor,
which yields pleasure equal to the difficulty.
Any mastery takes years. Any delivery to the other side
means thrashing across a current. I believed that the seeds
I planted would never sprout (they do for everybody else).
Until they did sprout by slim hairs of green.
Then became beans. Then tomatoes and winter cabbage.

Last of His Tribe

There will be a shack in the linden trees of Slovenia,
or in the chicory of Belgium, or amid spruces of the Siberian taiga,
or on a weedlot in Oakland. The ruined effort of the last human,
who will die next winter. No friend around to recite a prayer.
Or to cook meat in the old way, with spring onions and goose fat.
No child to occupy the small skin bed in the sleeping circle.
No one left to study the last language.
Or to remember the colors of the birds now extinct.
The size of this presses on the man,
the last witness of wind.

Late Winter

The afternoon sun is 100,000,000 lumens of radiant flux
igniting the pine trees in my retinas.
Gem-green mosses are 3000 lumens
padding the greywacke and schist.
Drooping heads of toothworts are 200 milk-white lumens—
clusters of light amid thick buckbrush.
Between 80 and 300 lumens emanate from various glowing,
odorous mushrooms bulging through oak-duff.
900 lumens is this human face reflecting
the mountain's lesser and greater lights.
50 lumens radiate the rufous-sided towhee I bend to see
scratching under a leafless bush.
One-fortieth of a foot-candle is a single firefly
emerging from the windy pines.
80,000,000 lumens sizzle
in the coruscating creek.
8,000 lumens are the hop tree's newborn triplet leaves,
one of which I pinch to smell what the sun has been doing.
Beneath the mud—not one packet or wave of light.
My feet slip on that darkness.

Mercy

My dead father is in the next room.
Mercy that there is no more of him to die.
I am still a collection of molecules that makes sense
in the rain. I do not dissolve.
I am glued together by affection
for wind and for people who have grown
endless varieties of baroque shells
around their soft parts.
My father has nothing to offer me
about what it is to be non-physical,
or if there is anything left over
except what is in the dreams of his son.
When my time is done, I think that my molecules will crackle
and go flat like a broken TV.
A shower of freed particles seeking new organizing principles.
Mercy that there is a rock five million years old
made up of silts and shells that I can stand next to in the wind.

Acknowledgments

Hayden's Ferry Review, Marsh Hawk, Genesis West, Sporklet, Periodicities, Marin Poetry Center Anthology. Some poems appeared in a chapbook, "I Say Your Name"—hand-set in letterpress by Lisa Rappoport at Littoral Press. Jack Gilbert, *z"l,* was my mentor and friend for fifteen years. His blessing to me before he died was simple: "Take your place." Marcia Falk, my *havruta,* without whom, nothing. Suzan Rood Wilson, my sister, the only witness. Rusty Morrison, partner in the art; Larry Felson, brother in the art. Linda Elkin, sister in the art. Liza Flum, sister in the art. C.S. Giscombe, brother in the art. Ken Keegan, brother in the art. Joe Landon, *bruder in die kunst.* Harvey Malloy, *bruder.* Tom McCorgray-Mallon, *z"l, frater.* Neil Russack, *z"l,* and John Beebe, alchemists. Amy Thomas, sister in the art. Donald Brees; Susan Bumps; Lucy Day; Mike Edwards; Suzanne Finney; J.K. Fowler; Helen Friedland, *z"l;* Hillel and Rachel Furstenberg; John Goodman; Judah Holstein, *z'l;* Joyce Jenkins; Mike Jones; Tony Keppelman; Audrey King; Sonia King; Mazisi Kunene, *z"l;* Norman Kurtin; Laura Lane; Jim LeCuyer; Lee Chulbum, *z"l;* Nancie Lualhati; Henry Lyman; Adrian Marriage, *z"l;* Laura Magnani; Bill Mayer, *z"l;* Thom, Virgil, and Francis McCorgray-Mallon; Lexi Potter; Lisa Rappoport; Edith and Jack Robinson, *z"l;* David Rollison; Lee Rossi; The San Francisco Ballet; Arthur Schmidt; Richard Silberg; Joe Smith; Elinor Stanley, *z"l;* Barbara Strauss, *z"l;* Barry Tagrin; Selma Turetzky, *z"l;* Wang Kap-ju, *z"l;* Yair and Val Zakovitch; Bonita Zisla.

Steven Rood was born in Los Angeles, attended Hollywood High School and the University of California, Berkeley, and is a practicing trial lawyer. He has studied classical guitar for decades. For 15 years he was a friend and poetry student of Jack Gilbert, until Jack's death. An earlier iteration of the manuscript for this book was a 2019 National Poetry Series Finalist. His poems appear in *Periodicities, Sporklet, Quarterly West, Marin Poetry Center Anthology, Fugue, Lyric, Hayden's Ferry Review, Tar River Poetry, New Letters, The Marlboro Review, The Atlanta Review, The Southern Poetry Review, Notre Dame Review,* and elsewhere. He lives in Berkeley with his spouse, the poet and Jewish Feminist liturgist, Marcia Falk. Their son, Abraham, teaches high school English in Oakland to newly arrived immigrants from Mexico and Central America.

Naming the Wind
Steven Rood

Cover Photo by John Kleinhans

Cover typefaces: Albertus MT Std & Garamond Premier Pro.
Interior typefaces: Bernhard Modern & Garamond Premier Pro

Cover and interior design by Ken Keegan

Printed in the United States
by Books International, Dulles, Virginia
On Glatfelter 50# Cream Natures Book 440 ppi
Acid Free Archival Quality Recycled Paper

Publication of this book was made possible in part by gifts from
Katherine & John Gravendyk in honor of Hillary Gravendyk,
Francesca Bell, Mary Mackey, and The New Place Fund

Omnidawn Publishing
Oakland, California
Staff and Volunteers, Spring 2022

Rusty Morrison & Ken Keegan, senior editors & co-publishers
Laura Joakimson, production editor and poetry & fiction editor
Rob Hendricks, editor for *Omniverse* & fiction, & post-pub marketing,
Sharon Zetter, poetry editor & book designer
Liza Flum, poetry editor
Matthew Bowie, poetry editor
Anthony Cody, poetry editor
Jason Bayani, poetry editor
Gail Aronson, fiction editor
Jennifer Metsker, marketing assistant